Quentin Blake

Tell Me a Picture

This book was originally published to accompany an exhibition at
The National Gallery, London
14 February – 17 June 2001

First published in Great Britain in 2001 by
National Gallery Company Limited

This edition first published in 2015 by Frances Lincoln Children's Books
This new paperback edition published in 2016 by Frances Lincoln Children's Books
74–77 White Lion Street, London N1 9PF
QuartoKnows.com
Visit our blogs at QuartoKnows.com

ISBN 978-1-84780-765-6

British Library Cataloguing in Publication Data
available on request

Printed in China

Cover picture: Pietro Longhi, Exhibition of a Rhinoceros at Venice, about 1751

Cover artwork: Quentin Blake

1 3 5 7 9 10 8 6 4 2

Quentin Blake

Tell Me a Picture

Adventures in looking at art

Frances Lincoln
Children's Books

in association with National Gallery Company, London

In memory of Stanley and Cynthia Simmonds

Author's acknowledgements

Tell Me a Picture would not have been possible without the support and
enthusiasm of the Education department of the London National Gallery.
I owe thanks to all the staff of the Gallery and in particular to Ghislaine Kenyon,
whose collaboration included not only providing most of the notes on individual
paintings but also helpful discussion of every aspect of this book.

When, in 1999, I was appointed the first Children's Laureate, my task was to encourage people (young people, but not only them) to take an interest in books – both in their words and in their pictures. That was why I was very pleased when the National Gallery agreed that I could be the curator of an exhibition called Tell Me A Picture.

My idea was to show, side by side, pictures by illustrators and by modern painters as well as some of the old master paintings already in the National Gallery. What they would have in common would be that each picture would have some kind of story in it. I arranged them in alphabetical order, so that no one picture was treated as more important than another. I wanted the people looking at the pictures to have their own thoughts about them without being told in advance what they ought to be.

I was also invited by the Director of Exhibitions at the National Gallery at the time, Michael Wilson, to do something that I would never have thought of suggesting, which was to draw on the walls. I don't think you are generally allowed to do that – and in fact my drawings were not really drawn on the walls but printed on transparent acetate so that they could be stripped off afterwards. It meant that I could introduce a collection of children who accompanied you round the exhibition and told you the name of the artists. Some of them have got into this book, where they do that job and also make comments of their own. They are really there to start you off with your own thoughts and observations, which I am sure are going to be a lot more interesting than theirs.

All the pictures in this book are ones I like, and if you like them too you may eventually want to know more about them and the artists who created them, so there are some notes about the artists, when they lived and how they worked, at the end of the book.

In the title of this book I have referred to "adventures" in looking at art. I certainly found it very exciting to look for the pictures that are included in this book – and there are so many pictures in the world, so many thoughts and feelings that we can have about them and so much pleasure in looking at them, that I really do feel it is a kind of adventure. I hope you will too.

Quentin Blake

Can you see that man who has fallen over?

I hope they don't fall through that hole in the ice.

It makes us feel chilly.

A

The first picture is by Avercamp

7

Wherever it is they've got terrible weather.

I wonder where they're off to.

This picture is by John Burningham

I think it looks exciting.

9

C

This picture is by Emma Chichester Clark

I wonder what's in all those parcels.

Is it his birthday?

I think they're presents.

If they are he doesn't look very pleased to get them.

I think it
looks a bit
dangerous.

Where's he
off to?

D
This picture is by
Daumier

Perhaps it's magic.

That is the <u>cleverest</u> monkey I have ever seen.

How do you think he does it?

F

This picture is by Michael Foreman

I don't know
what's happening
but it looks
really bogey.

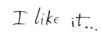

G

This picture is by Goya

I like it...

This picture is by Edward Hopper

Do you think he's waiting for someone?

Perhaps he's all alone.

Perhaps he just likes a bit of peace and quiet.

Do you think he knows about those two in the corner?

My friend used to live in a house exactly like that.

I

This picture is by Roberto Innocenti

He doesn't
look very happy.
I wonder
why not.

Clowns are
like that
sometimes.

K

This picture
is by
Ken Kiff

M

This picture is by Monticelli

Perhaps they're going to stay up all night.

What sort of party is that do you think?

I think it would
be a good place to explore.

Do you think
anyone lives there?
It looks
a bit broken.

Do you think
there are
my ghosts?

This picture
is by de Nomé

O

This picture is by Emily Mary Osborn

She does look rather sad. I wonder what the picture is.

Do you think he's going to buy it?

Come along, don't worry. It isn't real.

All the same...

Why do you think they're asleep?

Sometimes I do gardening like that.

I think a pelican is the best bird in the whole world.

R This picture is by Paula Rego

Is that a real fight or a sort of play?

S

This picture is by Gabriel de Saint-Aubin

43

T

This picture is by Giovanni Domenico Tiepolo

What a lovely horse.

Are they building it or are they trying to break it?

I think it looks fun.

The lady
doesn't look
very worried.

Well I feel
sorry for
the dragon.
What has it
done to
deserve that?

U

This
picture is by
Paolo
Uccello

I don't think you
should treat anyone's
pet like that.

Are they going
on their holidays?

Anyway,
we do.

I'm not sure
animals have holidays.

I think
it looks like
a ghost!

X

This picture is an
X-ray photograph
of a still-life painting
by Harmen Steenwyck

Z

This picture is by Lisbeth Zwerger

I'm famous for the way I cook baked beans on toast.

Burnt sausages are my speciality.

My speciality is eating.

Notes on the Paintings

Hendrick Avercamp
(1585–1634)
A Winter Scene with Skaters near a Castle
p.7
Painted in about 1608–9,
measures 40.7 cm in diameter

This painting is full of small stories. Among the people out on the ice, look out for a man begging, a couple colliding and another man fixing a woman's ice-skate.

Hendrick Avercamp was born in Amsterdam. He lived in a town called Kampen in the northern Netherlands, and was known as 'the mute of Kampen' because he could not speak. He painted busy winter scenes and made coloured drawings of people he might have come across in everyday life, such as farmers and fishermen.

John Burningham
(1936–)
From *Oi! Get off our Train*
p.9
Published in 1989

In this dramatic picture a small boy and a dog drive a steam train along a wooden bridge over water. Under a cloudy, moonlit sky they leave the city behind at the start of a dream-like adventure.

John Burningham is one of the best-known and most highly regarded of current British illustrators. His other books include *Mr Gumpy's Outing*, *The Shopping Basket*, *Granpa*, *Borka* and *Simp*.

Emma Chichester Clark
(1954–)
A Love Affair
p.11
Painted in 1997, measures 160 x 220 cm

The tall figure of a woman offers a heap of presents to a boy, but he seems reluctant to accept them. Instead he leans against the tree holding a cigar and looking up suspiciously.

Emma Chichester Clark is a successful illustrator of children's books including *I Love You, Blue Kangaroo* and *The Best of Times*, by Michael Morpurgo.

Honoré-Victorin Daumier
(1808–1879)
Don Quixote and Sancho Panza
p.13
Painted in about 1855,
measures 40.3 x 64.1 cm

Don Quixote was an extraordinary knight who had some bizarre adventures, as told by the seventeenth-century Spanish author Miguel de Cervantes. Here, Don Quixote is charging at a flock of sheep, believing it to be the enemy.

Honoré-Victorin Daumier lived in Paris for almost all of his life. He made his living illustrating newspapers that commented on the political and social life of the time.

Adam Elsheimer
(1578–1610)
Saint Paul on Malta
p.15
Painted in about 1600,
measures 16.8 x 21.3 cm

The Bible tells the story of how a terrible storm shipwrecked Saint Paul, who in the picture is wearing a red-lined cloak, on the Mediterranean island of Malta. As Paul threw sticks onto the fire a snake darted out and bit his hand, but when he shook off the snake the islanders saw he had not been hurt and believed him to be a god.

Adam Elsheimer was born in Germany but settled in Rome, where he became famous for his night landscapes.

Michael Foreman
(1938–)
From Seasons of Splendour
p.17
Published in 1985

This picture tells the story of an Indian folk tale in which the monkey Hanuman is on a mission to the Himalayas in search of special healing herbs to revive the prince-god Ram's wounded army. The monkey arrives at the mountains at nightfall and can't tell which plant is which. Rather than pick the wrong one, he decides to take the whole mountain to the army instead.

Michael Foreman is one of the most well known children's illustrators working today. His books include *War Game* and *The Amazing Tale of Ali Pasha*.

Francisco de Goya
(1746–1828)
A Scene from El Hechizado por Fuerza
('The Forcibly Bewitched')
p.19
Painted in 1798, measures 42.5 x 30.8 cm

This scene is from a seventeenth-century Spanish play. Doña Leonora wants to marry Don Claudio, but he resists until she frightens him with a trick. She makes him believe that her slave Lucía has bewitched him, and that he will only stay alive if the lamp in Lucía's room is kept alight. He is shown pouring oil into a lamp shaped like a ram.

Francisco de Goya was one of the most famous and admired Spanish painters. He became painter to the King of Spain in 1786.

Edward Hopper
(1882–1967)
Night in the Park
p.21
Made in 1921, measures 17.8 x 21.3 cm

This atmospheric picture – showing a man sitting on a park bench reading a newspaper – is one of a set of etchings by the same artist that show everyday aspects of contemporary American life.

Edward Hopper is one of America's most popular twentieth-century artists. He developed a style of composition involving flat masses of colour and large, simple shapes.

Roberto Innocenti
(1940–)
From The Adventures of Pinocchio
p.23
Published in 1988

This painting is an illustration of a scene of the classic children's book Pinocchio. The wooden puppet hero kneels before a house where the blue fairy appears at a high window.

Roberto Innocenti has illustrated many classic books including Charles Dickens's *A Christmas Carol*, Charles Perrault's *Cinderella* and E. T. A. Hoffman's *Nutcracker*.

David Jones
(1895–1974)
The Garden Enclosed
p.25
Painted in 1924, measures 35.6 x 29.8 cm

David Jones painted this picture to mark his engagement. The two figures embracing are the artist and his new fiancée, while around them trees wave their branches, and a flock of geese makes its way across the picture.

An artist and poet, David Jones studied at Camberwell School of Art in London and then fought in WWI. After the war ended, he returned to painting. His most famous work of poetry, *In Parenthesis*, was published in 1937.

Ken Kiff (1935–2001)
Clown
p.27
Made between 1996–9,
measures 50.5 x 54.5 cm

A figure dressed in a clown-like costume stands pointing towards the water, where a fish looks up at him. In the background another person holding a mallet or hammer climbs into the scene.

Ken Kiff drew, painted and made prints. He was born in Essex and went to Hornsey School of Art in London. From 1992–4 he was Associate Artist at the National Gallery.

Pietro Longhi (1700/2–1785)
Exhibition of a Rhinoceros At Venice
p.29
Probably painted in 1751,
measures 60.4 x 47 cm

The rhinoceros was a new and strange creature in Europe when this picture was painted. The one shown here was brought to Venice in 1751 for the annual carnival and was exhibited for the public to see.

Pietro Longhi worked in Venice. He painted small scenes of aristocratic and bourgeois life.

Adolphe Monticelli (1824–1886)
Torchlight Procession
p.31
Probably painted between 1870–86,
measures 30.5 x 48.9 cm

A celebration seems to be taking place in this picture. As fireworks explode in the sky, two of the richly costumed figures are having a conversation, while a man in white urges them onwards.

Adolphe Monticelli was born in Marseilles but studied in Paris. He spent many hours in the Louvre, learning from the works of artists such as Rembrandt, Titian and Jean-Antoine Watteau.

François de Nomé (about 1593–after 1630)
Fantastic Ruins with Saint Augustine and the Child
p.33
Painted in 1623, measures 45.1 x 66 cm

In this painting, the fourth-century Saint Augustine walks along the seashore meditating on the Trinity (of God the Father, the Son and Holy Spirit) when he meets a small child who is trying to empty the sea into a hole dug in the sand with a seashell. When Augustine remarks that this is an impossible task, the child replies that Augustine is doing something even more impossible by trying to explain the Trinity.

François de Nomé came from Metz in Eastern France, but worked in Rome and Naples in Italy. He painted mainly buildings and night-time scenes.

Emily Mary Osborn (1834–about 1893)
Nameless and Friendless
p.35
Painted in 1857,
measures 82.5 x 104.2 cm

A young woman artist has walked with a child (perhaps her son or her young brother) through the rain to an art dealer and is trying to sell her work. She seems to be poor and unmarried, as she has no wedding ring.

Emily Mary Osborn showed work at the Royal Academy in London when she was still a teenager. By 1855 she had important portrait commissions and she sold a picture to Queen Victoria.

Piero di Cosimo (about 1462–1522)

A Satyr mourning over a Nymph
p.37
Painted in about 1495, measures 65.4 x 184.2 cm

A seemingly lifeless nymph lies on the grass with wounded hand, wrist and throat. A kneeling satyr – half-goat, half-man – bends tenderly over her while a dog sits at her feet. This could be connected to the tale of Procris from Ovid's *Metamorphoses*, who was accidentally killed by her husband while he was hunting.

Piero di Cosimo was the son of a Florentine goldsmith. This picture was probably originally a backboard for a bench or chest or part of the panelling of a Florentine palace.

The Quay Brothers (1947–)

Serenato in Vano
p.39
Made in 1970,
measures 14.3 x 15.1 cm

Three strange musicians are shown playing on unusual old instruments. They have face-like masks but no heads. On the right an armoured figure raises its hands, but it has no arms.

The Quay brothers are twins. Since 1980 they have worked on a wide range of projects including puppet-animation and live-action films, as well as set designs for opera, theatre and ballet productions, and films for television.

Paula Rego (1935–)

Sleeping
p.41
Painted in 1986,
measures x 150 x 150 cm

According to the artist, this picture is about an episode in the Bible. Before Jesus was arrested and eventually crucified, he took three of his disciples to the Mount of Olives to pray. He walked a little way from them where an angel appeared to him. When he returned to the disciples they had fallen asleep. In this picture the disciples have become 'naughty girls'.

Paula Rego is one of the most distinguished contemporary figurative painters. She was born in Portugal and lives in England.

Gabriel-Jacques de Saint-Aubin (1724–1780)

A Street Show in Paris
p.43
Painted in 1760,
measures 80 x 64.1 cm

On this stage in a city street, two men fight a mock duel. Some of the audience seem more interested in their own private dramas than what is happening on the stage.

Gabriel-Jacques de Saint-Aubin lived and died in Paris. He made few paintings and is best known for his engravings and drawings.

Giovanni Domenico Tiepolo (1727–1804)

The Building of the Trojan Horse
p.45
Painted in about 1760,
measures 38.8 x 66.7 cm

The ancient Greeks laid siege to the city of Troy for nearly ten years. In a final attempt to gain access to the city they built a wooden horse in which they hid their troops. Here men are building furiously, working on the wooden structure with their hammers and chisels.

Giovanni Domenico Tiepolo was born in Venice, but he also worked in Würzburg in Germany and Madrid.

Paolo Uccello
(1397–1475)
Saint George and the Dragon
p.47
Painted in about 1470,
measures 56.5 x 74 cm

This picture tells a story from the legend of St George, who is said to have lived in the third century and was made patron saint of England in 1222. Here, St George is defeating a dragon who had been terrorising the inhabitants of a city, and rescuing a princess it had captured.

Paolo Uccello worked mainly in Florence painting pictures on wood panels, canvas and walls.

Gabrielle Vincent
(1928–2000)
From *Ernest est Malade*
p.49
Published in 1987

A mouse dressed in a child's clothes and an apron stands on a stool at an old-fashioned sink surrounded by kitchen disorder. The mouse is called Célestine. She and a bear called Ernest appear in a series of twenty-five books.

Gabrielle Vincent was a Belgian illustrator who illustrated numerous books, but is best known as the creator of *Ernest et Célestine*.

Józef Wilkon
(1930–)
From *Bats in the Belfry*
p.51
Published in 1985

This picture is from a book in which a fire forces a family of bats to leave their bell-tower home. As nocturnal (night-time) creatures, they are under pressure to find dark shelter before daybreak. Here they have spied an open attic window.

Józef Wilkon is one of the most famous Polish illustrators of books for young children. His books include *Flowers for the Snowman* and *The Story of the Kind Wolf*.

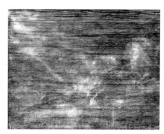

Harmen Steenwyck
(1612–1656)
X-ray of *Still life: An Allegory of the Vanities of Human Life*
p.53
Painted in about 1640,
measures 39.2 x 50.7 cm

This image is an X-ray of a painting. X-rays can help scientists discover how a painting was made by penetrating layers of paint to reveal ideas or plans the artist might have painted over. In this x-ray of a picture by the Dutch artist Harmen Steenwyck you can see a ghostly face under the bottle on the right. Steenwyck started by painting a bust or portrait, probably of a Roman emperor, but he must have changed his mind and painted a bottle over the top.

Jack B. Yeats
(1871–1957)
The Double Jockey Act
p.55
Painted in 1916,
measures 61 x 46 cm

Two bareback riders balance on a piebald horse that is cantering round the ring of a travelling circus. A clown gallops crazily alongside the horse, imitating both the men and the animal.

Jack Yeats was part of a great Irish artistic family. He painted in oils, specialising in landscapes and scenes of Irish life.

Lisbeth Zwerger
(1954–)
From *Dwarf Nose*
p.57
Published in 1993

A squat man with an enormous nose stands behind a huge metal tureen surrounded by ingredients and utensils. This bizarre figure with a copper frying pan and a shaker is watched by five doubtful-looking chefs.

Lisbeth Zwerger is an Austrian illustrator who received the Hans Christian Andersen Medal in 1990 for her contribution to children's books.

Where to find the pictures

A. Hendrick Avercamp, *A Winter Scene with Skaters near a Castle*, is from The National Gallery, London

B. John Burningham's picture is from the book *Oi! Get off our Train*, published by Jonathan Cape, 1989 (© John Burningham. Photo: The National Gallery, London)

C. Emma Chichester Clark, *A Love Affair*, is from a private collection (© Emma Chichester Clark. Photo: The National Gallery, London)

D. Honoré-Victorin Daumier, *Don Quixote and Sancho Panza*, is from The National Gallery, London

E. Adam Elsheimer, *Saint Paul on Malta*, is from The National Gallery, London

F. Michael Foreman's picture is from the book *Seasons of Splendour*, published by Pavilion, 1985 (© Michael Foreman. Photo: The National Gallery, London)

G. Francisco de Goya, *A Scene from El Hechizado por Fuerza ('The Forcibly Bewitched')*, is from The National Gallery, London

H. Edward Hopper, *Night in the Park*, is from The British Museum, London (© Photo: The British Museum, London)

I. Roberto Innocenti's picture is from the book *The Adventures of Pinocchio*, published by Jonathan Cape, 1988 (© Roberto Innocenti. Photo: Roberto Innocenti, Florence)

J. David Jones, *The Garden Enclosed*, is from the Tate, London (© Trustees of the David Jones Estate. Photo: Tate 2001)

K. Ken Kiff, *Clown*, is from Marlborough Graphics, London (© successors of Ken Kiff. Photo: courtesy of Marlborough Graphics, London)

L. Pietro Longhi, *Exhibition of a Rhinoceros at Venice*, is from The National Gallery, London

M. Adolphe Monticelli, *Torchlight Procession*, is from The National Gallery, London

N. François de Nomé, *Fantastic Ruins with Saint Augustine and the Child*, is from The National Gallery, London

O. Emily Mary Osborn, *Nameless and Friendless*, is from a private collection (© Emily Mary Osborn. Photo: courtesy of the owner)

P. Piero di Cosimo, *A Satyr mourning over a Nymph*, is from The National Gallery, London

Q. The Quay Brothers, *Serenato in Vano*, is from a private collection (© The Quay Brothers. Photo: The National Gallery, London)

R. Paula Rego, *Sleeping*, is from the Arts Council Collection, Hayward Gallery, London (© Paula Rego. Photo: courtesy of the Arts Council Collection, Hayward Gallery, London)

S. Gabriel-Jacques de Saint-Aubin, *A Street Show in Paris*, is from The National Gallery, London

T. Giovanni Domenico Tiepolo, *The Building of the Trojan Horse*, is from The National Gallery, London

U. Paolo Uccello, *Saint George and the Dragon*, is from The National Gallery, London

V. Gabrielle Vincent's picture is from the book *Ernest est Malade*, published by Duculot, 1987 (© Gabrielle Vincent. Courtesy of Casterman Editions, Brussels. Photo: The National Gallery, London)

W. Józef Wilkoń's picture is from the book *Bats in the Belfry*, published by Bohem Press Kinderverlag, 1985 (© Józef Wilkoń. Courtesy of Bohem Press, Zurich. Photo: The National Gallery, London)

X. Harmen Steenwyck, *Still Life: An Allegory of the Vanities of Human Life*, and its X-ray, are from The National Gallery, London

Y. Jack B. Yeats, *The Double Jockey Act*, is from The National Gallery of Ireland, Dublin (© Successors of Jack B. Yeats. Photo: National Gallery of Ireland, Dublin)

Z. Lisbeth Zwerger's picture is from the book *Dwarf Nose*, published by North-South books (© Lisbeth Zwerger. Photo: courtesy of Nord-Süd Verlag, Zurich)

All pictures © The National Gallery, London unless otherwise stated

About the Author

Quentin Blake was born in 1932. He read English at Downing College, Cambridge; Education at the London Institute of Education and attended life classes at Chelsea School of Art. He taught Illustration for over twenty years at the Royal College of Art. His first illustrated children's book appeared in 1960, and since then he has worked on over 300, collaborating, among many other writers, with Russell Hoban, Michael Rosen, John Yeoman and, most famously, Roald Dahl. He is also known for his own picture books such as *Clown* and *Zagazoo*, and his illustrations to classics such as *Don Quixote* and *Candide*. In the past fifteen years he has also worked on many projects for museums, hospitals, and other public spaces. In 1999 he was appointed first Children's Laureate. He was knighted in 2013 for services to illustration, and he is also a chevalier of the Légion d'Honneur.